BY THOMAS K. ADAMSON

THE BUFFALO
BILLS
STORY

BELLWETHER MEDIA · MINNEAPOLIS, MN

TM

Are you ready to take it to the extreme? Torque books thrust you into the action-packed world of sports, vehicles, mystery, and adventure. These books may include dirt, smoke, fire, and chilling tales. **WARNING** : read at your own risk.

This edition first published in 2017 by Bellwether Media, Inc.

No part of this publication may be reproduced in whole or in part without written permission of the publisher. For information regarding permission, write to Bellwether Media, Inc., Attention: Permissions Department, 5357 Penn Avenue South, Minneapolis, MN 55419.

Library of Congress Cataloging-in-Publication Data

Names: Adamson, Thomas K., 1970- author.
Title: The Buffalo Bills Story / by Thomas K. Adamson.
Description: Minneapolis, MN : Bellwether Media, Inc., 2017. | Series:
  Torque: NFL Teams | Includes bibliographical references and index.
Identifiers: LCCN 2015045493 | ISBN 9781626173583 (hardcover : alk. paper)
Subjects: LCSH: Buffalo Bills (Football team)–History–Juvenile literature.
Classification: LCC GV956.B83 A53 2017 | DDC 796.332/640974797–dc23
LC record available at http://lccn.loc.gov/2015045493

Printed in the United States of America, North Mankato, MN.

TABLE OF CONTENTS

The Buffalo Bills are in Massachusetts to take on the New England Patriots. This is the Bills' last game of the 2014 season.

The Bills will have their first **winning record** in 10 years if they win. But the Patriots are favored for this game.

Kyle Orton

The Bills start strong. **Quarterback** Kyle Orton completes a 43-yard pass to **wide receiver** Sammy Watkins in the first quarter. Then Orton hits wide receiver Robert Woods for a touchdown. The Bills take the lead!

In the second quarter, Anthony Dixon pounds in a 1-yard touchdown run. The Patriots cannot keep up. The Bills get the win 17 to 9.

Robert Woods

SCORING TERMS

END ZONE
the area at each end of a football field; a team scores by entering the opponent's end zone with the football.

EXTRA POINT
a score that occurs when a kicker kicks the ball between the opponent's goal posts after a touchdown is scored; 1 point.

FIELD GOAL
a score that occurs when a kicker kicks the ball between the opponent's goal posts; 3 points.

SAFETY
a score that occurs when a player on offense is tackled behind his own goal line; 2 points for defense.

TOUCHDOWN
a score that occurs when a team crosses into its opponent's end zone with the football; 6 points.

TWO-POINT CONVERSION
a score that occurs when a team crosses into its opponent's end zone with the football after scoring a touchdown; 2 points.

The Buffalo Bills charged to the top of the American Football **Conference** (AFC) from 1990 to 1993. They won four AFC Championships in a row for those seasons!

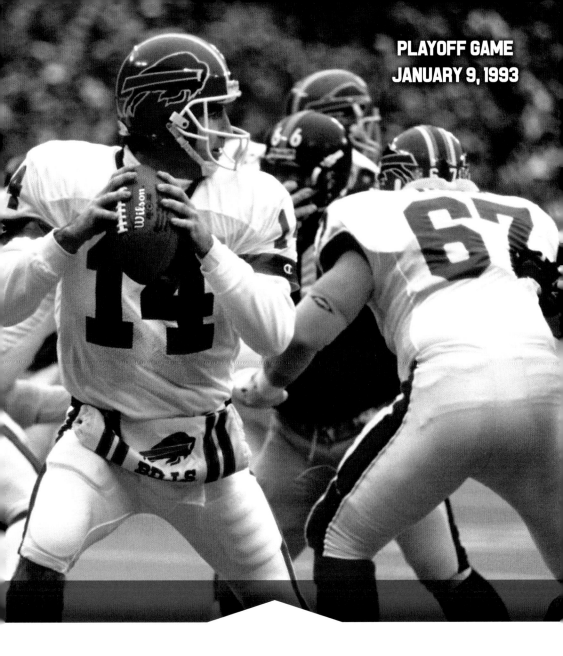

Fans remember the Bills' powerhouse team in the 1990s. They had a winning record in all but two seasons back then.

ROCKPILE

The Bills first played in War Memorial Stadium in Buffalo. It was nicknamed "The Rockpile."

The Bills play their home games at Ralph Wilson Stadium in Orchard Park, New York. The stadium is just outside Buffalo.

The field is 50 feet (15 meters) below ground level. This gives fans a great view. But it can also cause swirling winds. Visiting teams have trouble with the windy weather!

ORCHARD PARK, NEW YORK

The Bills play in the AFC East **Division**. The Miami Dolphins are their biggest **rival**. The Bills had a 20-game losing streak against the Dolphins in the 1970s.

But the Bills have overpowered them in the **playoffs**. As of 2016, they have won three out of four playoff games against the Dolphins!

NFL DIVISIONS

AFC

AFC NORTH

BALTIMORE **RAVENS**

CINCINNATI **BENGALS**

CLEVELAND **BROWNS**

PITTSBURGH **STEELERS**

AFC EAST

BUFFALO **BILLS**

MIAMI **DOLPHINS**

NEW ENGLAND **PATRIOTS**

NEW YORK **JETS**

AFC SOUTH

HOUSTON **TEXANS**

INDIANAPOLIS **COLTS**

JACKSONVILLE **JAGUARS**

TENNESSEE **TITANS**

AFC WEST

DENVER **BRONCOS**

KANSAS CITY **CHIEFS**

OAKLAND **RAIDERS**

SAN DIEGO **CHARGERS**

NFC

NFC NORTH

 CHICAGO
BEARS

 DETROIT
LIONS

 GREEN BAY
PACKERS

 MINNESOTA
VIKINGS

NFC EAST

 DALLAS
COWBOYS

 NEW YORK
GIANTS

 PHILADELPHIA
EAGLES

 WASHINGTON
REDSKINS

NFC SOUTH

 ATLANTA
FALCONS

 CAROLINA
PANTHERS

 NEW ORLEANS
SAINTS

TAMPA BAY
BUCCANEERS

NFC WEST

 ARIZONA
CARDINALS

 LOS ANGELES
RAMS

 SAN FRANCISCO
49ERS

 SEATTLE
SEAHAWKS

The Buffalo Bills were one of the original members of the American Football League (AFL) in 1960. They won back-to-back AFL Championships in 1964 and 1965.

In 1970, the AFL joined the National Football League (NFL). Soon after, the Bills had many losses. They worked toward a brighter future.

1964 season

The Bills were considered the best team in the NFL during the 1990 season. They went to their first **Super Bowl** in 1991. They only lost by a field goal.

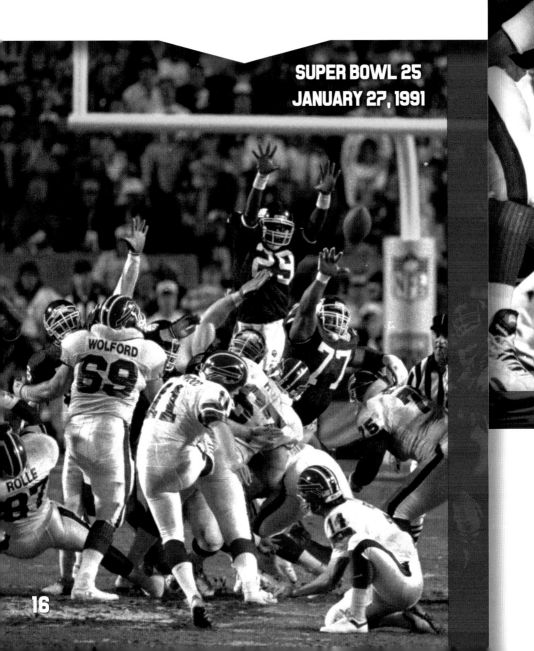

SUPER BOWL 25
JANUARY 27, 1991

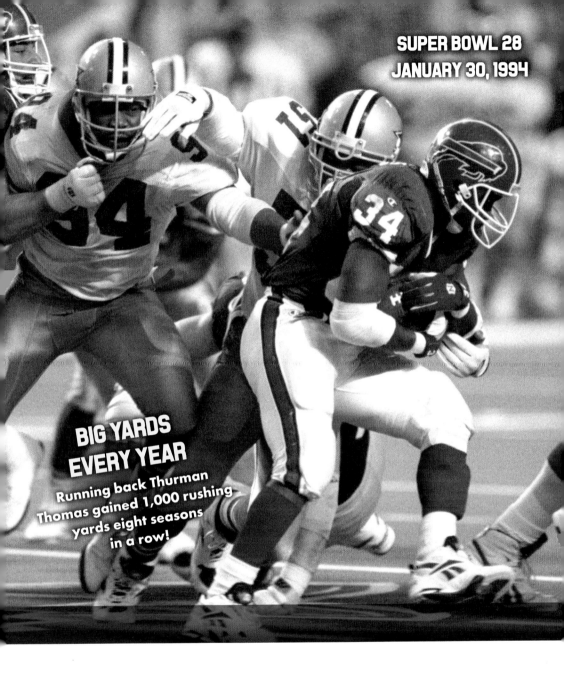

**BIG YARDS
EVERY YEAR**

Running back Thurman
Thomas gained 1,000 rushing
yards eight seasons
in a row!

The team fought their way to the next
three Super Bowls. This set an NFL record for
most Super Bowl appearances in a row!

TIMELINE

1965

Won their second straight AFL Championship, beating the San Diego Chargers (23-0)

1974

Replaced logo of a red standing buffalo with a blue charging buffalo

1959

Granted as an AFL franchise

1960

Played first regular season game, but lost to the New York Titans (now the New York Jets) (3-27)

1973

Played first regular season in what is now called Ralph Wilson Stadium

1994

Played in their fourth straight Super Bowl, but lost to the Dallas Cowboys

 13 FINAL SCORE **30**

2015

Signed quarterback Tyrod Taylor

2016

Hired Kathryn Smith as a special teams coach; she is the NFL's first full-time female coach.

1991

Won their first AFC Championship, beating the Los Angeles Raiders (now the Oakland Raiders) (51-3)

Joe DeLamielleure was a **guard** in the 1970s. He blocked for **running back** O.J. Simpson. Simpson was the first player to run over 2,000 yards in a 14-game season.

Andre Reed

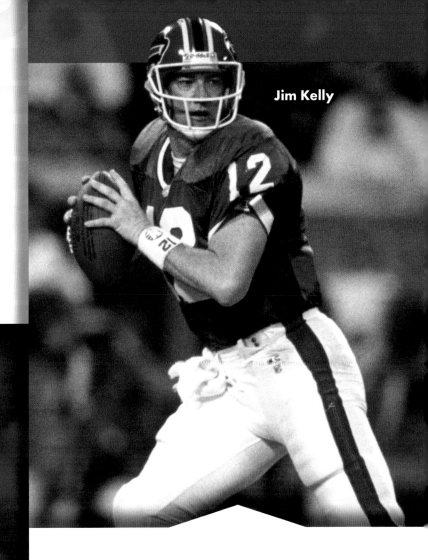

Jim Kelly

Andre Reed was a key
wide receiver during the
Bills' Super Bowl years.
Quarterback Jim Kelly led
the "no-huddle" **offense**.
This wore down the other
team's **defense**.

The Bills have had some great **defensive linemen**. Fred Smerlas led the team in the 1980s. He went to the **Pro Bowl** five times.

Bruce Smith got at least 10 **sacks** in 12 of the 15 seasons he played for the Bills. He also forced 35 fumbles.

TEAM GREATS

JOE DELAMIELLEURE
GUARD
1973-1979, 1985

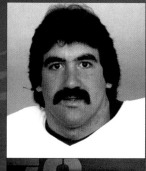

FRED SMERLAS
NOSE TACKLE
1979-1989

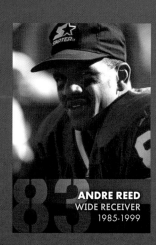

ANDRE REED
WIDE RECEIVER
1985-1999

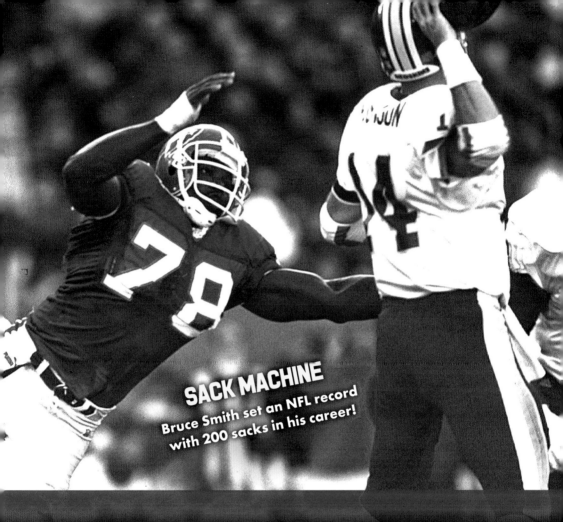

SACK MACHINE
Bruce Smith set an NFL record with 200 sacks in his career!

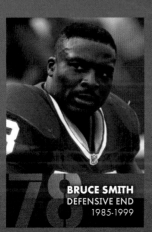

BRUCE SMITH
DEFENSIVE END
1985-1999

JIM KELLY
QUARTERBACK
1986-1996

THURMAN THOMAS
RUNNING BACK
1988-1999

Bills fans are as tough as Buffalo's cold weather. The coldest game ever played in Buffalo was a playoff game on January 15, 1994.

Bills fans packed the stadium. The Bills won against the Los Angeles Raiders (now the Oakland Raiders) 29 to 23!

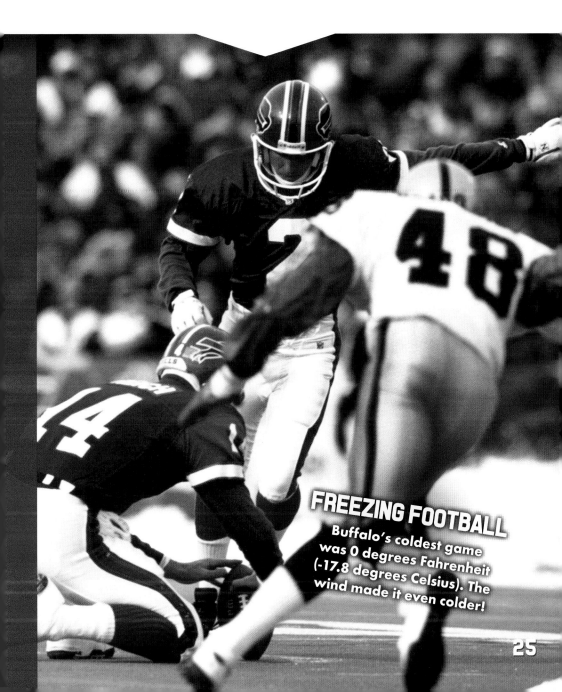

FREEZING FOOTBALL
Buffalo's coldest game was 0 degrees Fahrenheit (-17.8 degrees Celsius). The wind made it even colder!

The Bills' pregame parties may be the best in the NFL. Fans get one another pumped for the game. They talk about the greatest comeback in NFL history.

In 1993, the Bills made a 32-point comeback. They beat the Houston Oilers (now the Tennessee Titans) 41 to 38 in overtime! Fans cheer for the Bills' next great comeback and winning streak.

MORE ABOUT THE
BILLS

Team name:
Buffalo Bills

Team name explained:
Named after William F. "Buffalo Bill" Cody

Nicknames: The Electric Company, Bermuda Triangle

Joined NFL: 1970 (AFL from 1960-1969)

Conference: AFC

Division: East

Main rivals: Miami Dolphins, New England Patriots

Hometown:
Buffalo, New York

Training camp location:
St. John Fisher College, Pittsford, New York

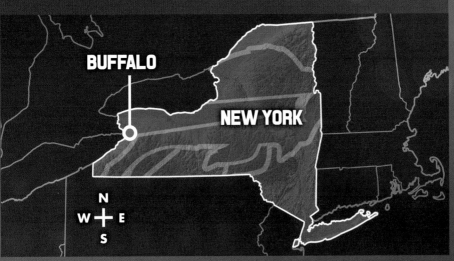

BUFFALO

NEW YORK

N
W + E
S

Home stadium name:
Ralph Wilson Stadium

Stadium opened: 1973

Seats in stadium: 73,079

Logo: A blue charging buffalo with a red streak

Colors: Blue, white, red

Mascot: Billy Buffalo

GLOSSARY

conference—a large grouping of sports teams that often play one another

defense—the group of players who try to stop the opposing team from scoring

defensive linemen—players on defense whose main job is to try to stop the quarterback; defensive linemen crouch down in front of the ball.

division—a small grouping of sports teams that often play one another; usually there are several divisions of teams in a conference.

guard—a player on offense whose job is to tackle the linemen of the opposing team

offense—the group of players who try to move down the field and score

playoffs—the games played after the regular NFL season is over; playoff games determine which teams play in the Super Bowl.

Pro Bowl—an all-star game played after the regular season in which the best players in the NFL face one another

quarterback—a player on offense whose main job is to throw and hand off the ball

rival—a long-standing opponent

running back—a player on offense whose main job is to run with the ball

sacks—plays during which a player on defense tackles the opposing quarterback for a loss of yards

Super Bowl—the championship game for the NFL

wide receiver—a player on offense whose main job is to catch passes from the quarterback

winning record—when a team has more wins than losses in a season

TO LEARN MORE

AT THE LIBRARY

Gilbert, Sara. *The Story of the Buffalo Bills*. Mankato, Minn.: Creative Education, 2014.

Robinson, Tom. *Buffalo Bills*. Edina, Minn.: ABDO Pub., 2011.

Wilner, Barry. *Buffalo Bills*. Mankato, Minn.: Child's World, 2015.

ON THE WEB

Learning more about the Buffalo Bills is as easy as 1, 2, 3.

1. Go to www.factsurfer.com.

2. Enter "Buffalo Bills" into the search box.

3. Click the "Surf" button and you will see a list of related web sites.

With factsurfer.com, finding more information is just a click away.

INDEX